MILITARY AIRCRAFT

F-16
FIGHTING
FALCON

BY JOHN HAMILTON

VISIT US AT
WWW.ABDOPUBLISHING.COM

Published by ABDO Publishing Company, PO Box 398166, Minneapolis, MN 55439.
Copyright ©2012 by Abdo Consulting Group, Inc. International copyrights reserved in all countries. No part of this book may be reproduced in any form without written permission from the publisher. A&D Xtreme™ is a trademark and logo of ABDO Publishing Company.

Printed in the United States of America, North Mankato, Minnesota.
112011
012012

Editor: Sue Hamilton
Graphic Design: Sue Hamilton
Cover Design: John Hamilton
Cover Photo: U.S. Air Force
Interior Photos: All photos United States Air Force except: AP-pg 12; Corbis-pg 23; Getty Images-pgs 18-19 & 20-21.

ABDO Booklinks
Web sites about Military Aircraft are featured on our Book Links pages. These links are routinely monitored and updated to provide the most current information available. Web site: www.abdopublishing.com

Library of Congress Cataloging-in-Publication Data

Hamilton, John, 1959-
   F-16 Fighting Falcon / John Hamilton.
      p. cm. -- (Xtreme military aircraft)
   Includes index.
   ISBN 978-1-61783-268-0
   1. F-16 (Jet fighter plane)--Juvenile literature. I. Title.
   UG1242.F5H3556 2012
   623.74'64--dc23
                              2011042337

TABLE OF CONTENTS

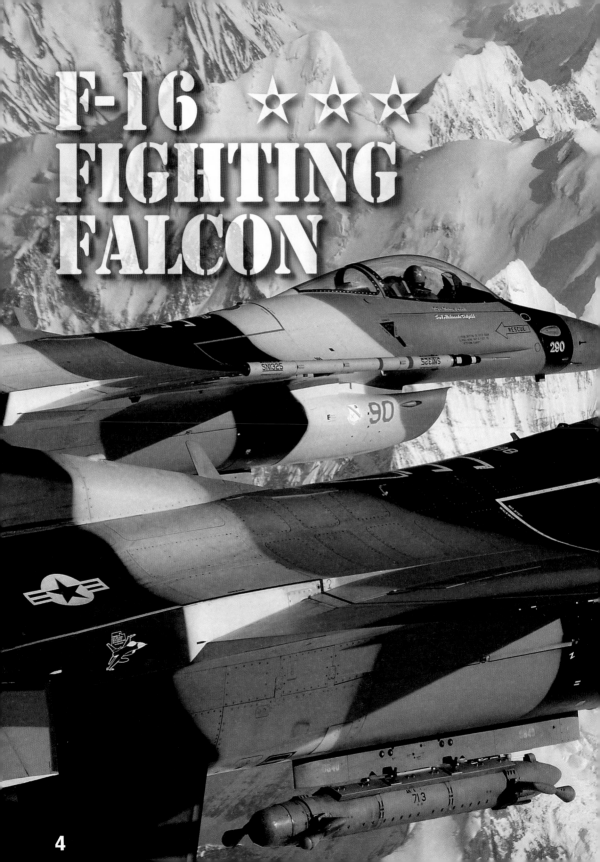

F-16 ☆☆☆
FIGHTING
FALCON

The F-16 Fighting Falcon is a multirole fighter jet. It is flown by the United States Air Force and Air National Guard. It is one of the best fighter jets in the world. It has many strengths and a successful combat record. The F-16 is a dangerous foe for any enemy in the air or on the ground.

F-16 Fighting Falcons in the U.S. Air Force's 18th Aggressor Squadron act as enemy planes during pilot training games. They are specially painted in gray, black, and white colors.

XTREME FACT

Thousands of F-16 Fighting Falcons have been built for the United States and its allies. Today, there are about 1,280 F-16s flown by the United States Air Force.

MISSION: AIR-TO-AIR

The F-16 Fighting Falcon excels at fighting enemy aircraft. It is very fast. It is also very maneuverable. The F-16 is designed to turn quickly. It can even fly straight up to gain altitude.

XTREME FACT

The F-16 can fly at Mach 2, twice the speed of sound. Its fastest speed is about 1,500 miles per hour (2,414 kph).

Being fast and turning quickly is important in air-to-air combat. Pilots can more easily fire their weapons at their foes, or escape enemy attacks.

MISSION: AIR-TO-GROUND

The F-16 Fighting Falcon is a multirole fighter. It can attack other planes. It can also attack enemy ground forces. The F-16's radar finds targets even in bad weather.

An F-16 Fighting Falcon fires a Sidewinder missile at a target drone.

With a full load of bombs and missiles, the F-16 can fly more than 500 miles (805 km) to attack enemy ground targets. It can defend itself against enemy planes, and return safely to base.

F-16 FIGHTING FALCON FAST FACTS

The F-16 Fighting Falcon is a very nimble aircraft. It can withstand up to nine G's, which is nine times the force of gravity. This is more than most other fighter aircraft.

F-16 Fighting Falcon Specifications

Function:	Multirole attack and fighter aircraft
Service Branch:	United States Air Force
Manufacturer:	General Dynamics/ Lockheed Martin
Crew:	One (F-16C) or two (F-16D)
Length:	49 feet, 5 inches (15 m)
Height:	16 feet (4.9 m)
Wingspan:	32 feet, 8 inches (10 m)
Maximum Takeoff Weight:	37,500 pounds (17,010 kg)
Airspeed:	Mach 2-plus (1,500 mph (2,414 kph) at altitude)
Ceiling:	50,000-plus feet (15,240 m)
Combat Range:	1,740 nautical miles (2,002 miles, or 3,322 km)

NICKNAME

The F-16's official nickname is "Fighting Falcon."
However, many pilots refer to the plane as
"Viper." The front part of the F-16 resembles a
snake. Some pilots also think the F-16 looks like
the Viper spacecraft from the television show
Battlestar Galactica.

*A scene from TV's
Battlestar Galactica
showing a Viper spacecraft
in an asteroid field.*

Skilled pilots show the maneuverability of their F-16 Fighting Falcons as part of the U.S. Air Force's Thunderbirds squadron.

ORIGINS

After the Vietnam War, the United States Air Force needed a new fighter jet. It wanted a plane that was lighter, more maneuverable, and had advanced electronics and weapons. The test plane, the YF-16, was built by aircraft manufacturer General Dynamics.

In 1976, the U.S. Air Force held a "Name the Plane" contest for the F-16. Technical Sergeant Joseph Kurdell's winning entry of "Fighting Falcon" was inspired by the Air Force Academy's mascot, the falcon.

XTREME FACT

The YF-16 was tested and modified for several years before plans for the F-16 were complete. The first F-16s were delivered to the Air Force in January 1979.

A YF-16 completes its first flight over Edwards Air Force Base in California in February 1974.

PILOTS

F-16 pilots are highly skilled and educated. They are Air Force officers with college degrees. Many have degrees from the United States Air Force Academy in Colorado Springs, Colorado. The smartest and most physically fit are considered for flight school.

An Air Force pilot makes a vertical climb in his F-16 Fighting Falcon.

Air Force pilots train for many years. This difficult training makes Air Force pilots some of the most skilled in the world. Only the very best pilots are chosen to fly F-16s.

COCKPIT

The F-16 Fighting Falcon uses advanced electronic fire-control systems in the cockpit. A head-up display in front of the pilot projects flight and combat information onto a transparent screen.

The F-16 cockpit is enclosed by a bubble canopy. The canopy has no metal frame. This gives the pilot an unobstructed forward view. The pilot also has improved vision to the sides and rear.

The F-16 pilot seat is angled 30 degrees. This extra incline helps pilots tolerate heavy gravity pull, or G-forces, when dogfighting enemy planes.

FLY-BY-WIRE

F-16 pilots fly the aircraft with a side stick controller. It is mounted on the right armrest of the seat. (Most other planes use center-mounted sticks between the pilot's legs.)

The F-16 uses a fly-by-wire flight control system. Hand pressure on the stick controller is detected by computers. This information is sent by electrical signals to devices called actuators. These devices move flight control surfaces such as rudders and ailerons, which help steer the plane.

Fly-by-wire flight control systems replace the usual system of cables and linkages that are used to control older, less-advanced aircraft.

ENGINE

The F-16 is a single-engine aircraft. It uses a Pratt & Whitney F100-PW-200 afterburning turbofan engine. Afterburners are used to give engines an extra boost of speed during takeoffs or in combat.

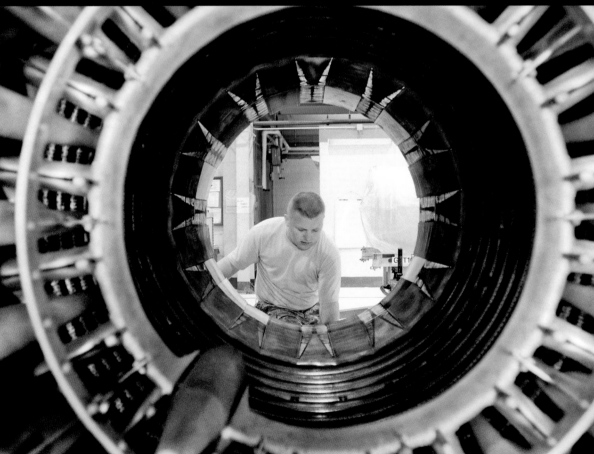

A senior airman examines the engine of an F-16 Fighting Falcon.

The F-16's engine produces large amounts of thrust. This results in more speed and the ability to carry more weapons.

The F-16 engine can produce up to 27,000 pounds of thrust (120,102 Newtons). Because of its powerful engine and light weight, the aircraft can fly straight up if necessary. This is called a "vertical climb," or "zoom departure."

WEAPONS

The F-16 can carry out many kinds of attacks. It has 11 places, called hardpoints, to mount missiles, bombs, and other equipment. It can carry up to six air-to-air missiles, such as the AIM-9 Sidewinder. It can also carry AIM-7 Sparrow and AIM-120 AMRAAM medium-range air-to-air missiles, as well as other air-to-ground missiles, rockets, and bombs.

XTREME FACT

The F-16 can be equipped to carry extra fuel in special pods mounted to hardpoints. It can also carry pods that have electronics that jam enemy radar.

The F-16 also has an M-61A1 20mm Vulcan cannon built into the front part of its left wing. This machine-gun-like weapon has a firing rate of 6,000 rounds per minute.

COMBAT HISTORY

An F-16 armed with AIM-9 Sidewinder missiles takes off from Saudi Arabia during Operation Desert Storm.

In 1991, the United States Air Force used F-16s in combat in the Persian Gulf during Operation Desert Storm. The aircraft were used to attack enemy airfields, missiles, and other targets. F-16s have also been used extensively during the U.S.-led wars in Iraq and Afghanistan. F-16s have successfully destroyed enemy radar sites, vehicles, tanks, and other military targets.

An F-16 on patrol over Afghanistan.

F-16s are also used to regularly patrol the shores of the United States. These anti-terrorism missions are part of Operation Noble Eagle.

An F-16 flies near the Florida coast.

THE FUTURE

The F-16 Fighting Falcon is no longer in production for the United States military. The Air Force plans instead to begin using the new F-35 Lightning II multirole fighter starting around 2016-2018.

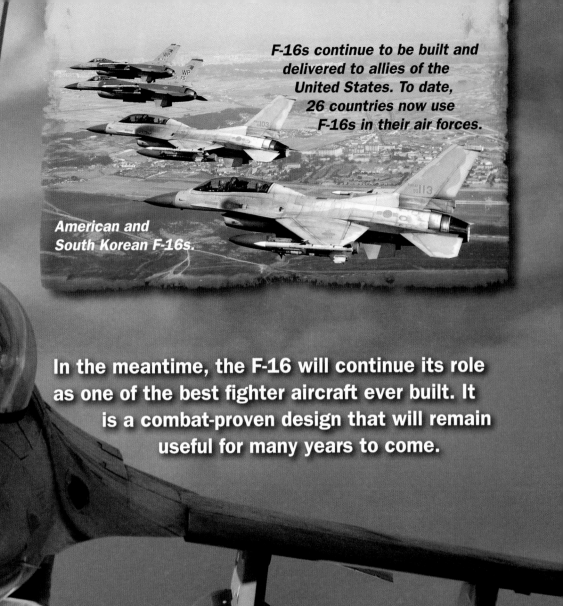

F-16s continue to be built and delivered to allies of the United States. To date, 26 countries now use F-16s in their air forces.

American and South Korean F-16s.

In the meantime, the F-16 will continue its role as one of the best fighter aircraft ever built. It is a combat-proven design that will remain useful for many years to come.

GLOSSARY

MACH
A common way to measure the speed of an aircraft when it approaches or exceeds the speed of sound in air. An aircraft traveling at Mach 1 is moving at the speed of sound, about 768 miles per hour (1,236 kph) when the air temperature is 68 degrees Fahrenheit (20 degrees C). An aircraft traveling at Mach 2 would be moving at twice the speed of sound.

MULTIROLE
Able to perform more than one task or mission. The F-16 is a multirole aircraft. It can attack enemy targets in the air or on land.

NAUTICAL MILE
A standard way to measure distance, especially when traveling in an aircraft or ship. It is based on the circumference of the Earth, the distance around the equator. This large circle is divided into 360 degrees. Each degree is further divided into 60 units called "minutes." A single minute of arc around the Earth is one nautical mile.

OPERATION DESERT STORM
Also called the Persian Gulf War. A war fought from 1990-1991 in Iraq and Kuwait between the forces of Iraq's President Saddam Hussein and a group of United Nations countries led by the United States.

Operation Noble Eagle

Military operations designed to protect the United States' homeland security. Security patrols, such as overflights by F-16s, are meant to support federal, state, and local law-enforcement agencies in their fight against terrorism. Operation Noble Eagle is a continuing effort that started in response to the September 11, 2001, terrorist attacks against the United States.

Pounds of Thrust

A way to measure the amount of force generated by aircraft engines (and other types of engines). The unit of measurement is usually in pounds (the metric equivalent is a unit called the Newton, named after the scientist Sir Isaac Newton). A pound of thrust is the amount of force needed to accelerate one pound of material 32 feet (9.8 m) per second every second (feet per second per second). One pound of thrust (32 feet per second per second) is the same as the acceleration of Earth's gravity.

Radar

A way to detect objects, such as aircraft or ships, using electromagnetic (radio) waves. Radar waves are sent out by large dishes, or antennas, and then strike an object. The radar dish then detects the reflected wave, which can tell operators how big an object is, how fast it is moving, its altitude, and its direction.

Vietnam War

A conflict between the countries of North Vietnam and South Vietnam from 1955-1975. Communist North Vietnam was supported by China and the Soviet Union. The United States entered the war on the side of South Vietnam.

INDEX